THE AGE OF LOCUST

Luis Carlos Molina Acevedo

Title: The Age of Locust

First Edition

Copyright ©1995 Luis Carlos Molina Acevedo

Second Edition

Copyright ©2016 Luis Carlos Molina Acevedo

©Texts: Luis Carlos Molina Acevedo

Author: Luis Carlos Molina Acevedo

Contact: lcmolinaa@yahoo.es

http://lcmolinaa.blogspot.com

Cover: Luis Carlos Molina Acevedo

Stile: Luis Carlos Molina Acevedo

All Right Reserved

ISBN-13: 978-1533030702

ISBN-10: 1533030707

About the Author

Luis Carlos Molina Acevedo is Social Communicator and Masters in Linguistics. The author has published the next books on online bookstores:

I Want to Fly, From Don Juan to Sexual Vampirism, The Imaginary of Exaggeration, The Clavicle of Dreams, For Writers by Writers, The Modern Concept of Communication, Is There Anybody Out The Wall?, Dr. House Syndrome, Zombie Factor, Magic: Symbols and Texts of Magic, Socio-semantics of Amity, and The Age of Locust.

Quiero Volar, El Alfarero de Cuentos, Virtuales Sensaciones, El Abogado del Presidente, Guayacán Rojo Sangre, Territorios de Muerte, Años de Langosta, El Confesor, El Orbe Llamador, Oscares al Desnudo, Diez Cortos Animados, La Fortaleza, Tribunal Inapelable, Operación Ameba, Territorios de la Muerte, La Edad de la Langosta, Del Donjuanismo al Vampirismo Sexual, Imaginaria de la Exageración, La Clavícula de los Sueños, Quince Escritores Colombianos, De Escritores para Escritores, El Moderno Concepto de Comunicación, Socio-semantics de la Amistad, Magia: Símbolos y Textos de la Magia, ¿Hay Alguien Afuera del Muro?, Síndrome Dr. House, y Factor Zombi.

Contend

Presentation

THE AGE OF LOCUST is a cultural essay about locust invasions in Colombia during the twentieth century. The biblical plague was a scourge to agriculture. It caused a great economic impact. The task of combating it was a civic and government work. Several programs were launched by the State to definitively eradicate it.

Locust invasions were strong during the first quarter century. By 1936 the last significant invasion occurred. Government programs were able to identify the origin of plague and progress towards eradication of it. In 1995, it turned to have news about the presence of the insect in the south of the country.

I must thank and to acknowledge the work of Camilo Calderon Schrader, who from his position as editor of "La Revista Credencial Historia" (the History Credential Magazine), contributed to the permanence of cultural, political and social memory of the country. His academic orientation was determined to make of national history a record of events, counted pleasantly and with academic rigor. Gone was cold and heavy style of history as a subject of classroom. He opened the space for the disclosure of the little-known aspects about the history of Colombia.

"La Revista Credencial Historia" has received important awards for its work. In 1992, it received the Commendation Simon Bolivar, from the National Ministry of Education, Colombia. In 1993, it was awarded with the National Prize of Journalism Simon Bolivar, for Best Cultural Work in Press. This magazine is monthly and has national circulation. In this, it was published for the first time "The Age of Locust" at number 63 on March 1995.

Biblical Plague Has Not Gone Away

It was first published in "La Revista Credencial Historia" (the History Credential Magazine), Bogota - Colombia, edition # 63, March 1995.

In April and May 1994, peasants in the department of Meta, Colombia, reported to the office of the Colombian Agricultural Institute, ICA, in Villavicencio, the presence of jumpy locust in the high plain. Since then, the Office of Prevention and Control has been monitoring the development of the plague. The locust was unable exceed the Meta river channel. In its flatlands, it is the increased presence of natural enemies of the plague, which are the best method of control. It has identified the heron as the most effective, next to the cowbirds, the Güerere, the curlews of flatland and carracos (birds native to the region).

Locust invasions in this century had a devastating effect on Colombian agriculture, creating economic disorders, social and political. In the southwest region of Antioquia, there are several oral testimonies about invasions in 1906, 1909, 1916, 1918-1920, 1926, 1928 and a passing in 1936. Of this, it is said, only the characteristic hum of the plague was heard during the flying and locust cloud in the sky was seen. It passed without settling this time in that region. It spent long ago elsewhere in the country.

The arrival of the locust involved hasty movement of livestock in search of other lands where he could eat, because the plague ended with pasture. Food was scarce, and there were consequent famines. "How would be the hunger that my younger brother, who at that time was two months old, the tip of the sole of a sandal he was eating, and if it is not because my mom saw him just at time, he eats it all," says Julian Bolivar, informant of the municipality of Betulia (Antioquia), Colombia. His testimony about the plague is poignant: "I was about eight years old. I went with my brother to the crop and when we did not expect it we heard a buzz and we went back to look and we found a flock of crickets came flying. We took machetes and began to burst them in the air. We were entertained killing them when the rain, of those animals, comes direct toward us, then we were frightened and we ran for the house. My mom was praying on her knees in the yard. The next day everything was peeling. The cassava patch was white branches because the locusts had eaten the crust. It was both the animals that corn plants bent down with them. We spent very hungry."

People had to go to the little vegetation left by the locusts to survive. The insect not eat corn cobs when they had reached their maximum maturity, or were "jechas" (a term used by people of southwestern of Antioquia, to refer to corn in its maturity), nor rascadera (other plant of the region) ate. This plant produces spicy milk, and leaves were used by the people as victual, beside the weeds of calabash to make soups (These plants are considered weeds among the inhabitants of the region). To give substance to this menu, in most cases tearing the doors to remove leather hinges. They threw them to the broth to give it some flavor (In peasant houses, hinges for opening and closing the doors were made of cow leather). In other cases, several families united and bought a femur beef commonly called "calabombo" or "hipbone" or "bone of substance" (this bone, in normal times, usually given away in butcher shops, or it was left for the stray dogs). Such bone was turned between them for days to spice up soups. The insects do not attacked also the coffee bushes, by the bitter taste of its leaves. They devoured the sweet corn (known regionally as "corncob"), cassava, bananas, beans, sugar cane, cotton, pineapple, papaya, oranges and other agricultural commodities.

The above testimonies speak about the predominant state of poverty, after the invasion of locusts. But the farmer was not worried about both the invasion itself, but the young left on the land. They hatched a few days and became an endless nightmare, because do not allow other action different the one of exterminating. The only work available in the haciendas was to catch the bugs to pack them in bags. The hatchlings began devouring the lower floors, but in a few days were able to climb higher. Their mature period could last up to two months, within which they were unable to fly to go and ate any new outbreak of vegetation. Any crop left by the invasion, it was then eaten by the offspring. It was useless to reseed because new specimens ravaged any crop, before flying up off the floor and leave.

The locust in Colombia

It is incredible to understand how an insect with only six teeth in each jaw, caused and continue to cause much terror to man. Its devastator power ruined the best crops in the past and it seems as if the same could happen again at any time in Colombia. Where it sat, from one day to another devoured the crops, they were large or small, and left only desolation. The locust is presented as a rather mysterious insect. While in isolated state, it is harmless, but when it develops its gregarious spirit, is as destructive as war.

At La Universidad Nacional (the National University), Medellin, Colombia, they were realized experiments with solitary locusts and after a few days of being together, they took the brown or dark gray coloration of the gregarious. That is, the locust in its natural state is greenish, similar to cricket, but when it is in the company of other locusts, it changed its green color to a blackish color, and when it migrates in herds, its color turns brownish. This insect has three colors: green, blackish and brown, depending on whether it is alone or in company, or if it has flown to other regions than the original one. This is a fact not yet explained by science and arouses curiosity. Color changes, presumably, must have some evolutionary sense.

Another novel experiments, made at the National University of Colombia, Medellin, was to separate, by a cut with a sharp knife, the trunk of the head. Then, it was stood beside its head, tender leaves of plants. For bewilderment of those present, the mutilated head devoured several leaves, despite being dismembered from body.

Since 1936 no locust invasions in Colombia are recorded and this is another point of wonder about this insect, because invasions in Brazil, Peru and other neighboring countries are prevalent today. According to historical data, invasions in Colombia were given most often from south to north. From that perspective, the country should be suffering the rigors of this plague, because these countries bordering with Colombia by the south.

In Colombia, it was identified as the center of origin, Cumbitira region, near the Patia River in the department of Cauca. Other researchers assigned also the Laguna del Castigo (the Lagoon of Punishment) as point of origin for this plague. This lagoon is located in the vicinity of the birth of Magdalena and the Cauca River. It took this name, in accordance with testimonies, because there were thrown some Franciscans at the time of the colony. They were killed, but before doing so, the monks launched a curse. Since then, his punishment is felt in the form of invasion of locusts.

The history of the Franciscans is not far from being influenced by the familiar biblical story (Exodus, 10: 13-15). There, we read how God, through Moses punished the Egyptian people, given the refusal of Pharaoh to let out the Jewish people to the Promised Land. Another version of the origin of the plague in Colombia poses a similar hypothesis, but without the religious accent. For this, locust, of New Granada, lived in the desert of "The Punishment", located on the banks of the Patia River, near the mouth in the Pacific Ocean. The name is preserved, but here is no longer a lagoon, but a desert. Usually, the insects got out of there every 6, 8 or 10 years. Sometimes, they migrated toward the south and others toward north over Popayan (a city), and followed the course of the Cauca River. From 1814 to 1815, it spreads throughout the Valle del Cauca to the parish of San Andrés in the province of Antioquia.

Apparently the locust existed for many years in Colombia and perhaps was confined to the Amazon River in the jungle. It may not feel the need to leave the thick vegetation of that region. The first reference to it, out of the jungle, is recorded in Pasto at 1619. This historical fact is known, because the inhabitants decided to adopt, as a protector against locusts, to the saint Fray Luis Beltran. The destruction of this plague has been very powerful and can only appeal to divine power to counter it. In 1748, it is also said, Father Larre, in Popayan, conjured it in the name of San Joaquin. By then, the plague had advanced to the north of the country.

In 1916 the locust invaded 16 sections of the country. In addition, Antioquia records another in

1909 with equal magnitude. However, since 1878 the expansion of the plague was denounced in the Bulletin of Trade. From this print newspaper, it is already crying out to the national government on the need to undertake programs to eradicate locusts. There were strong invasions in 1906 and 1908 from the department of Bolívar. These invasions attract attention because they seem to get away from the normal flight pattern of the plague, which was from south to north. Assuming as origin the birth of the Magdalena River, according to historical records, then the locust arrived at the department of Bolívar and returned.

In Santa Fe de Antioquia, a municipality of the department of Antioquia, Colombia, they came to attack until costumes of the laundresses (name given to women when washing clothes on the banks of rivers) and thatched roofs (Dwellings instead of roofs, using dry branches of iraca or thatch Panama, plant whose branches resemble to the one of palm trees). It affected several towns in western, southwestern and lower Cauca of Antioquia between 1918 and 1920, especially in the dry months (midyear). It is commonly called as chapulinas, pacu-pacos and jumpers (they are really names given to locust, depending on the degree of development). They are high and compressed body, head of equal width, transverse grooves and varied coloration. At first glance, they can be confused with a cricket, but they are a little larger.

The problem of locust invasion became very large. The national government enacted legislative controls to force governors and mayors, to take action to exterminate the plague. The first was the Law 19 on October 17, 1911. Article 15 provided fines of 2-20 Colombian Peso for negligence in the extermination of locust. These were very heavy fines for that time, when it is compared with the wages paid by then. These were valued in cents (one hundredth of a Colombian Peso).

Law 65, on November 9 of 1914, regulated the fumigation of the origin point of the plague, that is, Desert or Lagoon of Punishment. This law was enacted, when several research groups at universities were able to identify that place as the source of the plague. Fumigation proposed was based on an application of arsenic in proportion of 200 pounds of arsenic per 15 gallons of boiling water, plus five gallons of cold water and 40 gallons of honey from sugar cane. The interesting thing was how locally extermination measures were already long before. For example, in the department of Antioquia, it was the ordinance 32 on August of 1890 and Decree 145 on 28 April 1906, by which was provided the order to municipalities to fight locusts by all means. These orders must be met to avoid political sanctions.

The fighting against locust was not only government work. Science was also struggled to find more effective means to combat it. They deserve special mention the recommendations given in 1916 by agronomist Dawe, advisor, by that then, to the Ministry of Agriculture. He designed a strategy of a system of trenches or pits (a vara of wide by a vara of deep; vara is a unit of measure equal to 81 centimeters), in the lands invaded by locusts. Against the wall of the trench, a protruding edge table was installed. Against it, the locusts crashed and were being stacked on the bottom of the trench. When there were a lot of them, they were covered with soil. This was the system most used by the farmer of Antioquia, as it was recorded in the testimony of oral tradition.

Among the methods of extermination, portable traps with oil emulsion were also recommended. When the locust fell into these traps, it was died by poison action of the oil emulsion. And the most common methods, but slower, was the one of killing them with tree branches, leaves of maguey or leather straps. It was the method most used by so-called "grabbers" who were paid for their craft. In the absence of work in times of invasion, several gangs of men dedicated to manually capture the bugs. They packed them in bags and then sold them by lumps to owners of large estates. Thus, they offset somewhat the lack of income.

In the oral tradition of the Antiochian southwest, there are stories according to which, for a day of harvesting locust was paid a cup of porridge and two cents. To men crews, they were joined other battlers. Pets are formed in a great help to destroy the locusts. The more "professional", in this business, was the pig. This animal nuzzled tireless in search of eggs put under the ground and had a great sense of smell to find them. They chewed them as if they were the favorite delicacy. Chickens collaborated also in the work. They fed tireless with bugs, but in telling of people, this had a big disadvantage: the meat of birds took unpalatable taste during the next twenty days. At this time, they preferred not to consume the meat of these birds. The dogs joined also to the great work of survival. They, like other animals, searched these insects for eating them. They had also side effects. They lost weight after eating them and lost hair gradually until dying. There were many animals in combat, blackbirds, jays, toches, mockingbirds, siriríes, rice, chamones, cirihuelos, carriquíes, earwigs, carpenters and tile (all common names for wild birds the Antiochian southwest).

Luis Carlos Molina Acevedo

Features of Locust

From biology, locust belongs to the class of insects, Orthoptera order, jumpers section, Acrididés family, grasshopper genus, species Acridium peregrinum, of which there is a kind Colombian Acridium, typical of Colombia, with notable differences from those of the neighbor countries. This species appeared by the end of 1888, as it was recorded in studies done about it. In addition to this, they were identified in the invasions, also three other common species in South America: the Migratory Schistocerca Paramensis classified by Walk Burm and perhaps most common in Colombia. The Tropinotus Rosulentus classified by Stal, and identified in the invasion of 1936, especially in western of Antioquia, in where it was done the biological record of the species. This invasion was less strong and therefore is considered a last lag of the great migrations. There is also the Bogotensis, classified by Scud and the Tropidacris Latre, classified by Illei Perty. The latter is also known by the nickname "donkey" because of its large size, compared to the others. It came to measure up to 15 centimeters long. It has yellow wings and white little tubercles in the chest.

The emergence of posture delayed three to four weeks and since then went through five stages before reaching adulthood. The pups were born wingless, greenish and the third day they were becoming black. Eight days after moving into a gray, on the twelfth day they appeared the first yellow spots. At fifty days the chicks reached maturity wings. And three months were visible yellow and red dots on black background. They preferred to feed grasses and could eat the fresh manure from horses. When flying, the wings produced a distinctive buzz. This development cycle shows why it was useless any attempt to cultivate the land after an invasion of locusts. The seeds could be mixed with locust eggs on earth. The first buds could appear while eggs were hatched, and bugs, in developing, find early plants, appropriate for his feeding.

It is considered to South American species with greater longevity. The average life is 67 days. The complete life cycle is 133-200 days, but may reach a year. Sizes vary between six and eight centimeters long. The egg laid under earth begins after ten to fifteen days of copulation, and an insect manages between six to eight positions with intervals of ten to fifteen days. This great playability makes this plague be so scary. Mating occurs between the months on November and February. Migrations are more frequent between April and May toward the north and northwest. And invasions are more frequents between September and December. Their flights can be of two types, either of dispersion or of concentration. The latter is the most devastating to crops.

The Age of Locust

The locusts require dry and hot weather because needs the heat of the sun to fly (its weak wings are energized with the sun). They require xeric vegetation (not like bitter plants). They require also land semiarid to facilitate the laying of eggs and intermittent rains for hatching of eggs. Despite these requirements, insects managed to do great harm to the agricultural economy of any country.

After a few hours of being mated, the female pierces the earth with his horns flows, without letting the male, and place the eggs in the cavity or in the perpendicular ovipositor of 60 mm. deep. When it was spawn, the female loses its strength and usually dies within hours and not far from where laid. The male is separated, flutters few days in the near site of the spawning, remains generally fixed at a single point, its flight is short and extreme weakness. Its membranous wing (membranous wings under the wings themselves), wings and legs are shedding until dying. As a natural enemy of the locust, it was identified the Cocobacillus Acridiorum, classified by Herelle. This bacillus introduces into its body and can destroy it.

People of the Antiochian southwest aged over 80 who were interviewed between 1986 and 1989, when talking about the locust made the sign of the cross and said with something of fear, "Let's hope that we do not return to live this again!" In them, there is direct evidence of what this biblical plague can do. Often, they were powerless over it. They could do nothing, only pray, asking to God his early demise.

According to Uvarov, the most famous specialist about locust, "the problem of the migratory locust is

Luis Carlos Molina Acevedo

caused by man himself. Misuse of land creates favorable conditions for this. Overgrazing, over-harvesting and continuous burning, for example, has been eliminating in vast areas the original vegetation, turning forests into open terrain where locust has been waking up very easily and develops dangerous populations". It seems as if this entomologist was describing the process of accelerated deforestation in Colombia, and with it, the breeding ground for the resurgence of the plague again and again.

Bibliography

HOSTNIG, Rainer. «Resurgimiento de una plaga: langostas migratorias». Medio Ambiente. Lima. (16): 10-12, enero, 1987.

APOLINAR MARIA, Hermano. «La langosta». Boletín de la Sociedad Colombiana de Ciencias Naturales, año XV, No 88, oct-nov, 1926. pp. 166-73.

POSADA, A. La langosta, estudios científicos. Medellín: Imprenta oficial, 1909. pp. 92-104.

YEPES RODRIGUEZ, Francisco. Anotaciones históricas sobre algunas de las apariciones de la langosta en Colombia y Antioquia. Medellín: Secretaría de Agricultura de Antioquia, VII, 1987.

Luis Carlos Molina Acevedo